*by Vellum LLC*

I0161124

# Inside-out Legal

*The better way*
*for Alaska's small businesses*
*to manage their legal risks*

*PO Box 221974 Anchorage, Alaska 99522-1974*
*books@publicationconsultants.com*
*www.publicationconsultants.com*

ISBN 978-1-59433-272-2
Library of Congress Catalog Card Number: 2012930732

Manufactured in the United States of America.

# Contents

# Introduction

# *About Vellum LLC*

Inside-out Legal Services™ is the product of Vellum LLC, an Alaska law firm that aims to redesign legal services for the small business owner from the ground up. Vellum creates tools, services, and training for small business owners to manage and minimize their legal risks from start to finish. It's the Inside-out Legal way.

## Legal Tools

We've designed legal tools at Vellum to help you do most of the legwork on your own (this saves you lots of money and keeps costs down). You'll go online, answer questions, and get the forms and documents you need. Your attorney at Vellum will be available to help you during the whole process.

Vellum's philosophy is simple: with the right tools and learning resources you can get yourself to the twenty yard line. Your Vellum lawyer can then take you the rest of the way for a touchdown.

## Legal Services

It's common for small businesses to wait to engage an attorney until things have gone really bad, which can be costly when all you have are expensive law firms who charge you by the hour. But Vellum helps you take a more preventive approach where you can ask legal questions, ask for legal review, request legal forms, and get guidance in big decisions. This helps prevent the really bad stuff from happening.

## Learning Centers

In this day and age business owners don't hesitate to use the internet to learn things. You can find just about anything on the internet, but it's often difficult to tell how good the information is. With our learning centers you can get the legal information you need to help you understand your legal risks. When you take the time to learn, you'll also be much better equipped when you meet with your attorney. That's what this book is for.

# About Inside-out Legal

Most likely you're either starting a business or you're running a small business right now. You might even be thinking about selling your business, but no matter where you're at in the life of a business, you have legal risks.

Managing these risks is hard work and easy to ignore. Most small business owners ignore them until something goes really bad, then they call a lawyer and find out how costly that approach can be.

What can you do to manage these risks? There are self-help books. But it takes a lot of time to read all the books required to understand and manage these risks.

You can use online services. But these services lack the help of a local attorney and normally provide one-size-fits-all solutions.

You can call an attorney from a traditional law firm. This is expensive and traditional law firms aren't equipped with the tools needed to manage legal risks. They're mostly good at reacting to legal problems rather than preventing them.

The solution: Inside-out Legal Services™:

- is a low-cost way to manage legal risks the same way large corporations do
- is about learning just enough law to be aware of what can harm a small business
- is about taking preventive measures
- can be your legal department

# *How to Get Started*

The Inside-out Legal way starts with introducing you to legal concepts, your legal risks, and how you can minimize those risks. You don't need to be a legal expert. You just need to be aware of these things.

### Structure Your Business

Choose the best business structure when you're starting up. It might be a sole proprietorship, limited liability company, or a corporation. Adapt your structure as your business grows. You might want to form another LLC to hold valuable assets.

Create and follow the governing documents for your business. Create intercompany agreements, if necessary. And transfer assets to your LLC.

### Set up and Manage Your LLC

If you have employees, a partner, contracts, or valuable assets, then form an LLC with the state of Alaska. Enter into an operating agreement that accounts for how many owners your business has, your management structure, your tax election, the right buy-sell provisions, and everything else you need to govern your LLC.

### Protect Your Trademarks

Choose a strong trademark for your products and services that doesn't violate someone else's trademark rights. Consider registering your trademark with the United States Patent and Trademark Office, then protect it.

## Get a Good Lease

If you lease space, get a good lease. Take the time to allocate the duties and liabilities fairly between you and the landlord. Make sure everyone understands each other's expectations going into the lease, then follow it. Don't just file it away and forget about it. If you do these things, you'll go a long way to avoiding nasty landlord/tenant disputes.

## Manage Your Employees

Avoid the legal pitfalls surrounding your employees by correctly categorizing your independent contractors, correctly designating your employees as hourly or salaried, implementing and following an employee handbook, protecting your employee's right to privacy, following wage and hour laws, preventing illegal discrimination, keeping your employees safe, and much more.

## Enter into a Buy/Sell Agreement

The unfortunate truth of any business is that it will experience its tragedies. There might be death, disability, bankruptcy, or divorce to disrupt life. Sometimes owners want out of the business or a group of owners may want to force one of the owners out.

The members or shareholders can plan for these possibilities with agreements such as a right-of-first-refusal, a forced sale, or an option to purchase. The plan includes a mechanism to set the purchase price and a way to fund a purchase. Without these plans, the members or shareholders may end up with unwanted partners, the inability to buy-out a member, or the inability to sell their interest in the business.

## Negotiate the Sale or Purchase of a Business

One of these days you'll realize that your business is all grown up. You'll need to decide what you want to do with the business. Do you want to sell it? Do you want to transfer it to your children? Do you want to close it? Do you want to merge it? You need to think through these things to prepare for them.

The typical sale involves an exchange of information under a confidentiality agreement, an investigation of the company, sometimes a letter of intent, then negotiation of the business sale agreement and the final closing.

## The Most Important Thing

Yes, there is the most important thing. Your children don't bring you pride by merely being in compliance with the law. They bring you pride when they adopt the values and lessons you teach them. You want them to have a good reputation. If they have a great reputation, that's all the better.

Make sure you transfer your standards and values to your business and employees, then live up to them. Convey them to your employees. Write them down in a code and teach the code to your employees. Provide a mechanism that allows for reports about chinks in your armor so that you can fix them. It's all about integrity.

# *Disclaimer*

Some things look so easy that it's tempting to say: I can do this myself. Remember, the experts make things look easy because they've had years and years of training and practice. The same is true with lawyers. They've had years and years of education and practice. They're the experts.

This book isn't trying to make you a legal expert. It's not here to guide you to a particular action. It's only trying to introduce you to legal concepts and inform you about the law. It doesn't know your situation. It won't ask you all the right questions. It will just provide you with general legal information. So take the time and learn as much as you can. If you do, you'll be much better equipped when you go to a lawyer. You'll have a better idea of what to ask and you'll better grasp difficult legal concepts.

The other thing to remember is that laws are constantly changing. Some information might be outdated.

Please don't take this personally, but just because we're giving you legal information in a book or allowing you to contact us electronically doesn't mean that you (the reader) and Vellum LLC (the law firm) are an item. Vellum is not your attorney until you sign a fee agreement or you pay for our services.

Also, Vellum doesn't do tax law. Have you seen how many tax laws there are? It takes a special type of person to know that stuff—people like CPAs and tax attorneys. We're not part of that special group. So if you have tax questions, go see one of those people who are part of that group.

# Structuring a Business

Sole Proprietorships and Partnerships
Corporations
Limited Liability Companies (LLCs)
Multiple LLCs

~

Congratulations! You're starting a business in Alaska. Or maybe you're an existing business and are growing. Or maybe you're one of those businesses that started up without giving any thought to your business structure.

Whatever the case, your structure either protects you or exposes you to liability. It can affect how much you pay in taxes. It affects how you work with other business owners. Sometimes it can make or break you.

How should you structure your business? Let's look at the number of businesses formed in Alaska in 2010 to see what others are doing. Here they are:

- 9,000 sole proprietorship or partnerships
- 624 corporations
- 2799 limited liability companies
- 10 limited liability partnerships
- 115 limited partnerships
- 25 professional corporations

It looks like most people are forming sole proprietorships, partnerships, corporations, or limited liability companies. The other types of entities are typically used for specialized purposes. Let's take a closer look at the popular entity types and see how you can use them in your business.

# Sole Proprietorships and Partnerships

Ahhh, the good life of sole proprietorship and partnerships. You just get your business license and you're good to go. No fees to pay to form it. No reports to file.

But there are downsides. All of your personal assets such as your home, cars, boats, savings, etc. are exposed if your employees or partners do anything wrong or a contract goes south. Your business assets such as your equipment, vehicles, and intellectual property are exposed when you do something wrong that's not connected to your business.

What does this mean? Generally if you're going into business by yourself, or are already a sole proprietorship, and don't have employees, business assets, and contracts, then it makes sense to be a sole proprietorship. If you have a partner, an employee, any contacts, or valuable business assets, then you should seriously consider forming an LLC or corporation. Yes, you can always buy insurance to cover these risks, but becoming an entity such as an LLC or corporation is probably the cheapest insurance you can buy.

A few other things to consider:

If you're a sole proprietorship or partnership and decide to sell your business, you can only sell its assets. If you die, then your business probably dies with you.

If you choose to do business in a name other than your own, then get a business license in that name. Then you sign things in your name doing business as your business name. This is called a d/b/a.

# *Corporations*

Corporations take more effort to set up than sole proprietorships. You must file papers with the state of Alaska to bring it to life. The state then gives you a certificate of incorporation which is like your corporation's birth certificate. The corporation is considered a separate person so long as you follow a number of corporate formalities to keep it alive.

As a separate person, the corporation may enter into contracts, own property, be sued, and do business. This means that your personal assets such as your home, savings, cars, etc. are protected from the acts of the corporation so long as you follow the formalities to keep it alive.

But the big downsides of corporations are: double taxation (the corporate tax and your individual tax—although the tax to the corporation is often zeroed out); less protection from creditors than an LLC; double taxation when you sell the business; and, the burden of keeping up with corporate formalities.

Should you set up a corporation? Let's just make this easy. Generally if you expect to go public, you'll probably need a corporation. You'll also want to check with your CPA to see if some of the corporate tax advantages apply to you such as retained earnings, tax-favored fringe benefits, and fewer restrictions for claiming losses. But most of these benefits apply to larger and very profitable companies, so if you're just starting up, a corporation doesn't make much sense. Which brings us to LLCs.

# *Limited Liability Companies (LLCs)*

It takes about as much effort to set up an LLC as it does to form a corporation. You file papers with the state of Alaska, the state gives you articles of organization which is like the LLC's birth certificate, and the LLC is considered a separate person so long as you make an effort to keep it alive.

As a separate person, the LLC can enter into contracts, own property, and do business. This means that your personal assets such as your home, savings, cars, etc. are protected from the LLC's acts, the acts of your employees, and the acts of the other owners of the LLC.

But unlike corporations, LLC's are not subject to double taxation. They can be taxed as a sole proprietorship, partnership, S Corporation, or C Corporation. LLC's also don't require formalities and provide you with something called charging order protection. There's almost no downside to LLCs other than maintaining good standing with the state of Alaska and following its operating agreement.

Generally if you're a small business and have a partner, sign contracts, have employees, or have valuable business assets, then you should form an LLC. As mentioned before, it's the cheapest insurance you can buy.

# *Multiple LLCs*

For most people, one LLC is enough. But sometimes it makes sense to have more than one LLC.

If you own major business assets like equipment, warehouses, machinery, vehicles, etc., then you might want to set up another LLC and transfer your business assets to it. The LLC that owns these assets is called a holding company. Your other LLC that does business with the public is called an operating company. Your operating company can then lease the assets from your holding company for market rates.

Why would you want to do this? If someone sues your operating company, the assets in your holding company are protected from that lawsuit.

There's another scenario where you might want to have more than one LLC. That's when you have two different lines of business. If you have separate divisions, do business in separate locations, run businesses in separate industries, then you might want to set up separate LLCs for each line of business. Then the liabilities in one operating company are protected from the other operating company.

There are some drawbacks to having LLC holding companies and multiple LLCs. You must treat each LLC as strangers. They must each keep separate books, separate bank accounts, separate employment agreements, etc. If they share overhead, then they need to have a shared services agreement or an inter-company agreement between the companies. You need to have documents transferring asset ownership to your other LLCs such as a bill of sale, warranty deed, assignment, etc. Then you need to have some sort of rental or lease agreement between your LLCs.

# All About LLCs

Types
Operating Agreements
Formation
Limited Liability
Charging Orders
Membership
Management
Disputes
Meetings
Records
Taxation
Standards
Maintenance
Dissolution

~

Generally, small businesses with employees, more than one owner, valuable business assets, or contracts should form an LLC rather than a corporation. So let's focus on LLCs.

To make this easier, let me introduce you to my good friend Mr. LLC. That's right, an LLC is a totally separate person in the eyes of the law. Mr. LLC was conceived, born, lives and dies just like a real living human being. It gets even better than that. Mr. LLC can buy things, sign contracts, own things, go to court, be sued, and do almost anything else a real live person can legally do.

Let's start with looking at the various types of LLCs.

# *Types*

Mr. LLC has many personalities depending on the number of owners, management, and taxation.

If you plan on having one owner in your business, then you're a single-member LLC. If you plan on having more than one owner, then you're a multi-member LLC.

If you plan on having all the owners involved in the day-to-day management of your business, then you're a member-managed LLC. If not, then you need to select your manager and your LLC will be manager-managed.

If you plan on having assets or employees that make you money, then you'll want to work with your CPA and probably elect to be taxed as an S Corporation to save on social security and medicare taxes. In some cases you may still elect to be taxed as a partnership, but you can arrange things to minimize these taxes. Otherwise you'll want to be taxed as a disregarded entity if you're a single member LLC or as a partnership if you're a multi-member LLC.

Once you've answered these questions, you'll want to draft an operating agreement.

# *Operating Agreements*

Your LLC is a separate person. So how does it make decisions? Who feeds Mr. LLC? What happens to the money Mr. LLC earns and the assets he owns?

The answer—the operating agreement. It's just a written agreement between the owners of the LLC to settle these matters. The people who own Mr. LCC (called the members) are the LLC's brain. Without a brain you can't survive and make decisions. They make its decisions and act on its behalf.

The operating agreement includes things about Mr. LLC's money, assets, membership, and day-to-day decision making. It includes how Mr. LLC's big decisions are made, how his records are kept, what his standards are, and how to resolve disputes. It can also include what happens when a member dies, is disabled, goes bankrupt, or gets divorced.

The members don't have to have an operating agreement to do this. If the members don't have an operating agreement, then Alaska's LLC statutes will decide how the brain functions. But if you want to control how the brain functions, then you'll need an operating agreement.

There's another aspect to consider. The process of negotiating an operating agreement is a great way to set everyone's expectations up front. It can help avoid surprises down the road. It's like a prenuptial agreement for the members and it's a whole lot easier to agree on things when everyone is happy and still in the honeymoon period, than when everyone is mad at each other. Remember, you're not locked into the agreement. The members can always agree to change the operating agreement as time goes on.

Do you still need an operating agreement if you're the only member? If you're the only member of the LLC, then you're the one making all the decisions. But if you don't have an operating agreement, the default rules still apply to you. Sometimes you'll have to show lenders and landlords your operating agreement. The operating agreement also helps ensure that your legal, tax, and financial structures are in place. An operating agreement serves as a good guidebook to maintain Mr. LLC. So it's not a bad idea to have an operating agreement even if you're the only member.

Finally, when it comes to operating agreements, there is no one-size-fits-all solution because there are many different types of LLCs. It's like getting a suit or a dress. When you walk into a store to buy a suit or a dress, they don't offer just one size of suit or dress. They have multiple suit or dress sizes that work for just about every body type. The same is true with LLCs. You need to make sure your operating agreement fits you right. There really is no one-size-fits-all solution.

# *Formation*

Let's talk about the mechanics of creating Mr. LLC. Here's how it works most of the time:

- Meet with your attorney and CPA to figure out your business structure and tax election
- Check your business name for any trademark violations
- Consider filing a securities exemption if you have more than one owner ($50)
- If you're a single member LLC, draft and sign your operating agreement. If you're a multi-member LLC, negotiate and sign your operating agreement. It's better to do this before you file anything with the state in the event that you're unable to reach an agreement
- File articles of organization with the state of Alaska and pay the filing fee ($250)
- File your initial biennial report
- Purchase a business license for your LLC ($50)
- Enter reminders for good standing requirements such as biennial report filings and business license renewals
- If you have more than one LLC, sign inter-company service agreements
- Transfer assets to the appropriate LLCs
- Open up bank accounts for your LLC, create the books for each LLC, capitalize the LLC with money, promissory notes, services., and other items to make sure that you protect and maintain the limited liability shield.

# *Limited Liability*

Mr. LLC stands there with a shield ready to protect your personal stuff like your home, car, savings accounts, boats, and other things from lawsuits and creditors. If someone sues you for something Mr. LLC's employee did and wins the case; if Mr. LLC signs a contract with another company and that company sues Mr. LLC for breach of contract; if one of the other members commits malpractice or is personally negligent; in all these cases Mr. LLC protects your personal stuff. Mr. LLC can be your best protector and defender.

This is pretty powerful stuff, but Mr. LLC can't protect you from everything. There's this big misperception that if you set up an LLC you automatically have all this super-powered protection from all lawsuits. That's not true. You're still liable for your personal misconduct. That's why it's always good to talk with your insurance agent to get insurance.

There's another thing that Mr. LLC can't protect you from and that's disputes between members or between members and managers. Once again it's a good idea to talk with your insurance agent about this. You'll also want to include some sort of dispute resolution procedure in your operating agreement to help resolve these disputes.

You'll also find that unless your LLC is financially sound, your bank, landlord, and others will require you to sign a personal guarantee. This allows that person to seize your personal assets to pay off your LLC's debts.

Overall Mr. LLC is pretty powerful, but I wouldn't call him superman. Sorry Mr. LLC.

# Charging Orders

Let's say someone sues you personally. If you lose that lawsuit, the plaintiff will want to get their money. They'll go after your home, cars, savings accounts, and other personal assets; they'll garnish your wages; but all they can get against your LLC ownership interest is a charging order. This means Mr. LLC's business assets are protected, unless they also name your LLC in the lawsuit and win a judgment against your LLC.

Here's how it works. The person with a judgment against you gets a charging order from the court. The charging order says that all the plaintiff can get against your ownership interest in the LLC are the profits that are distributed to you. That means the plaintiff can't take over your LLC and liquidate its assets to pay off the judgment.

This is pretty powerful protection. In fact Alaska's charging order protection is one of the best in the nation. Not only does it prevent judgment creditors from foreclosing on your membership interest, it also prevents the judgment creditor from getting a court order for directions, accounts, and inquiries. This means that if the manager of the LLC decides not to make profit distributions, the creditor can't get any money or information from the Alaska LLC. Another thing to remember is that you don't get this protection with a corporation. That's one of the main reasons to go with an LLC.

Now there is some case law in other states that do not give charging order protection to *single* member LLCs. There are some states that explicitly provide charging order protection to single member LLCs. Alaska's statute is silent on the matter and the courts haven't decided one way or the other.

# *Membership*

Shareholders own corporations. Partners own partnerships. The sole proprietor owns a sole proprietorship. So who owns Mr. LLC? Members do.

When you first created Mr. LLC you identified its members. The members contributed money, services, promissory notes, or assets to Mr. LLC to become a member. They own Mr. LLC.

The members have control over Mr. LLC according to the governance provisions in the operating agreement and the Alaska LLC statutes or both. The members make all of Mr. LLC's decisions or they delegate the decisions to a manager. If the members delegate decisions to a manager, they can reserve some of the decisions for themselves. These are called member matters and are normally big decisions such as buying or selling expensive assets, signing big contracts, hiring important employees, merging with another company, doing yearly budgets, and other similar decisions.

The members normally make these big decisions by voting. There are a number of ways the members can vote. They can require a majority vote, unanimous vote, or certain percentage of votes to make a decision. They can give one vote to each member or they can give votes proportionate to the member's ownership.

The members can also set up different classes of membership where each member has different rights. For example, some members may have governing rights while other members would have only a right to the profits.

Whether Mr. LLC succeeds depends largely on its LLC membership. When you started Mr. LLC you got to choose Mr. LLC's members. You might be the only member or your LLC might have multiple members. In either case you know the people you're going into business with when you started Mr. LLC.

But things might change as time goes on. A member might want to sell his interest. There is always the chance a member may die, become disabled, file for bankruptcy, resign, divorce, or any number of things that change membership. If you don't have an operating agreement, then these events can change Mr. LLC in unexpected ways.

That's why you'll want a good buy/sell agreement to set the triggers for the events such as rights of first refusal, the purchase price, and other clauses. We'll talk more about these in the chapter on buy-sell agreements.

# *Management*

Someone has to make the decisions on behalf of Mr. LLC. There are mainly two ways to structure the LLC's management: member management or manager management. Here's what these two management systems mean.

If all of the members have the authority to make Mr. LLC's day-to-day decisions and are authorized to act on his behalf, then Mr. LLC is member managed. In this structure all of the members generally have equal management rights.

If one or more members don't want management responsibility or if the members want to limit the power of some of its members, then the members appoint one or more of the members or a non-member manager to make Mr. LLC's day-to-day decisions. This is called manager-management.

If there is only one member, then that member can choose member management. But it's generally a good idea for that owner to chose herself to be the manager and to designate the LLC as manager-managed.

There's a lot of flexibility with the management of Mr. LLC. You can also structure it to be like a corporation with a board of directors and officers. You can also develop management committees. You can give your manager whatever title you want to give him or her. You may also pay the manager a salary and other benefits separate from the profit the member manager earns from Mr. LLC.

# *Disputes*

Most members get along. Most managers live up to the LLC's standards. Most LLCs hum-along just fine. The chances of harmony increase when the members communicate constantly and effectively, communicate their expectations, and are respectful.

But every now and then the LLC can't make up its mind. The members may not agree on a matter. A manager might not live up to the LLC's standards. A member might breach the operating agreement or the law. When any of this happens, your operating agreement tells you how to resolve the dispute.

## Dispute resolution

The first step is to try to resolve things on your own. If this doesn't work, then you may try to resolve things through mediation. If that doesn't work, then you have to file the matter in court. If you waived your right to a jury trial in the operating agreement, a judge will decide the matter for you. If you didn't waive this right, then a jury will decide the matter. You may also agree to arbitrate the dispute.

## Insurance

If you're a manager and don't live up to the LLC's standards, then you're personally liable to the other members for any damages they incur by your failure. If you're a member or manager and breach the operating agreement or the law, then you're also personally liable to the other members for the breach. The LLC can look into purchasing insurance to cover you as a member or manager for these claims.

## Coverage

Even though you're a member or manager in an LLC, someone outside of the LLC can still name you personally in a lawsuit. You'll have to pay for your defense and any judgment, unless the members agree to pay for these. You can ask the LLC to advance your litigation expenses for these claims.

# *Meetings*

Are you required by Alaska law to have meetings? Nope. But even though the law doesn't require meetings, you can choose to make meetings a requirement in your operating agreement.

If you do, then make sure that you have those meetings according to those requirements. Even if you're not required to have meetings, sometimes it makes sense to have them. If you're going to make some big decision, then it's a good idea to have a meeting, discuss the decision, vote on it, and record the decision in a resolution and record the meeting with minutes. This helps strengthen the corporate veil because it shows that you're operating the LLC as a separate entity.

It normally makes sense to have meetings when you have more than one member. If you just have one member, then you don't need to go through this process, but you still might record your thought processes for your records.

Here's one way to have a meeting:

- Give notice of the meeting to all the members.
- Prepare an agenda.
- Prepare resolutions in advance.
- Hold the meeting, call the meeting to order, declare a quorum, read minutes from the last meeting, vote to approve minutes, handle unfinished business, present reports, take votes, then adjourn the meeting.
- Prepare written minutes, sign resolutions, and place documents into the LLC record book.

Sometimes you can take action by written consent and forego the meeting.

# *Records*

It's a good idea to include a provision in your operating agreement requiring you to keep the following records related to the organization and operations of Mr. LLC:

- Full name and last known mailing address of every manager and member.
- Articles of organization (amendments and restated articles).
- The LLC's tax returns and financial statements for the last three years. If the LLC didn't file tax returns, then copies of the information given to members to file their tax returns.
- Operating agreements and amendments, including former operating agreements.
- Minutes of meetings and evidence of voting.

All members may inspect and copy records and books for any reason. They just need to ask the manager for a copy of the record. The manager needs to promptly provide members with the requested records or give members access to the record. But each member is still under a duty of confidentiality regarding the record. The operating agreement may modify these rights.

# *Taxation*

There's always a little confusion when it comes to LLC taxation. The IRS doesn't have LLC taxation. Instead, it lets you choose how Mr. LLC will be taxed.

He can be taxed as a sole proprietor, partnership, an S corporation, or a C corporation. So if you're the only owner of Mr. LLC you can choose to be taxed like a sole proprietor or an S corporation. If you have multiple members, you can choose to have Mr. LLC taxed as a partnership or an S Corporation and even a C corporation (it rarely makes sense to be taxed as a C corporation). You'll need to make sure that your operating agreement includes provisions that address certain tax issues depending on what tax selection you make.

There are also state tax regulations and social security taxes to take into consideration. You should talk with your accountant about your tax election. The choice you make may save you thousands of dollars or cost you thousands of dollars. For example, if you earn income from your capital investments or from the work of your employees, then you might want to consider choosing S corporation taxation.

# *Standards*

Mr. LLC has standards set by law and your operating agreement.

## Standard of Care

The law says that Mr. LLC's members and managers must perform their duties in good faith, in Mr. LLC's best interests, and with the care that an ordinarily prudent person in a like position would use under similar circumstances. Here are a few guidelines to help you meet this standard:

- If you don't know the answer, look to your advisors and other professionals for help.
- If you don't have the skills to accomplish something, hire someone who has the skills, or learn them on your own.
- If you know something that makes reliance on the professional's advice unwarranted, then don't rely on the advice.
- If you start to rationalize your behavior, or don't have an honest belief that something is in the company's best interest, then don't do it.
- If you have doubts about an action, talk with the other members and get their consent to take a certain course of action.

## Loyalty

You are part of a team and must be loyal to it. Here are some team rules:

- You can't be on two competing teams. You must pick one or the other. You can't compete against Mr. LLC.
- You must protect the game plan. Mr. LLC's information and documents help it succeed. You must keep them confidential.
- You must do things in the best interests of the team. If you're caught in the middle of a tug-of-war between your personal interests and Mr. LLC's interests, then you have a conflict. You'll either have to withdraw from the matter or get the consent of the other members to participate.
- You must use the LLC's property to benefit the team and not yourself. Don't use Mr. LLC's assets for personal use. Don't enter into transactions such as loans and guarantees with the LLC without the consent of the other members as required in the operating agreement.
- You must not take advantage of your status as a team member to the disadvantage of the team.

Overall, you must be up front and honest with the other members. You must disclose information that the other members need to know with respect to Mr. LLC's business and internal affairs. You must disclose things to the other members and let them decide what you can do.

## Good faith and fair dealing

Every contract, including your operating agreement, includes an implied duty of good faith and fair dealing. This means that you will not thwart the duties, policies, rights, and privileges established in your LLC's operating agreement or bend its rules. You'll do your best to live up to the expectations established in the operating agreement.

# *Maintenance*

It's now clear that Mr. LLC is a separate person. Its cash is not your cash. Its assets are not your assets. If you mix Mr. LLC's cash and assets with your personal cash and assets, then Mr. LLC might not be treated as a separate person. The same holds true with your other companies. Here's what you need to do to keep things separate.

## Bank Accounts

Open a bank account in Mr. LLC's name. If you contributed startup cash to Mr. LLC, then deposit this cash in the bank account. Use Mr. LLC's account for business purposes only. Don't take money from it for personal use.

## Transferring Assets

If you contributed startup assets to Mr. LLC, transfer these assets to Mr. LLC via a bill of sale, deed, or whatever other legal instrument is necessary to transfer the assets to Mr. LLC. Then use these assets for business purposes only.

## Bookkeeping

Open up separate books for Mr. LLC and keep track of all its finances as a separate entity. If you own other LLCs or companies, those entities must have their own books.

## Contracts

Enter into contracts in the name of Mr. LLC. Here's how you sign those contracts.

Your Company Name, LLC


By: [signature of manager or member]
Manager [or Member if you're member-managed]

## Doing Business

Make it clear to your customers, suppliers, and others that they are doing business with Mr. LLC and not you personally. You should include the LLC part of your business name on things such as business cards, invoices, stationary, etc. You can refer to the business as *My LLC*. Don't use the term partner; use co-member instead.

## Capitalization

Keep Mr. LLC well fed. Make sure he has enough equity from its members (money, property, loans, assets, cash flow, and other financial resources) to pay his debts when due.

## LLC to LLC Relations

Your LLC must treat your other LLCs and corporations like strangers. If they provide services to each other, they must have contracts between them with terms just like any other contract between strangers

## Biennial Reports and Updates

You file a biennial report with the state of Alaska every two years to tell them and the public who owns and is in charge of your LLC. This information is on the internet. If something changes between biennial reports, you need to let Alaska know about the changes. You also need to get a business license and make sure it gets renewed.

## Registered Agent

If someone wants to sue Mr. LLC, that person can't say "hey Mr. LLC, I'm going to sue you." So how do you talk to Mr. LLC? That's where the registered agent comes into play.

You designate an official person or another corporation to be Mr. LLC's ears. This can be your attorney, a law firm, yourself, or a registered agent company. They listen to the people who need to talk with Mr. LLC about legal stuff such as summons, complaints, and other legal notices. This is an important job because they will be the one to respond to the person talking to Mr. LLC. If they ignore them, Mr. LLC could end up with a default judgment or some other legal action against it.

# *Dissolution*

Yes, it's sad to say, but there may a come a time when Mr. LLC dies. The members normally make this decision; but sometimes the state or a judge will force its death. The members normally appoint someone to wrap up Mr. LLC's business, pay its debts, distribute the profits and assets, and file the documents necessary with the state to officially notify it of Mr. LLC's death. You also can do some things to cut off creditor claims after a certain period of time passes from Mr. LLC's death.

# Trademarks

Name
Search
Evaluate
Register
Protect
The Internet

~

If you've ever had to name one of your children you know how hard it is to come up with a good name. Imagine if you had to choose a name for your child that didn't cause any sort of confusion with someone else's name. That would make it even harder. That's what you're up against when you choose a trademark.

The first thing you normally do when you start your business is choose your business name. Your formal business name chosen when you formed your LLC, corporation, or sole proprietorship isn't automatically your trademark. It only becomes a trademark if you use it to market your goods or services. For example, Franchise World Headquarters, LLC is the corporate name for Subway. Their trademark is Subway because that's what they slap on their storefronts, their packaging, their advertising, and everything else. In some cases the corporate name is also a trademark. For example, Apple, Inc. is a trade name and is also a trademark along with their other trademarks such as iPod, iPad, iPhone, etc.

A trademark is any word, design, slogan, sound, or symbol that serves to identify your product or services.

The steps to establishing federal trademark rights are as follows:

- Choose a good trademark and evaluate its strength.
- Conduct a trademark search.
- Evaluate the results of the search.
- Use the trademark in interstate commerce.
- Register the trademark with the United States Patent and Trademark Office (USPTO).
- Protect and renew the trademark.

The person or company who first uses the trademark in commerce automatically has rights to the trademark within the geographic scope of that use. They don't have to do anything else. If they use the trademark in one city, they have rights to the mark in that city. If they use it in two states, they only have rights to it in those two states. If they use it throughout the United States, they have rights to the trademark throughout the United States. These are called common law rights.

As soon as a person or company uses a trademark in more than one state, they may register the name with the USPTO. When the USPTO approves the application, the person or company has nationwide rights to the name regardless of the geographic scope of the use. Each state also has its own trademark registration system to gain rights to the mark in that state. Most people cut to the chase and just get the federal registration. Once you've established rights in the trademark, you need to take steps to protect it.

# *Name*

Some names don't receive any trademark protection and some are stronger than others. Let's run through an example to see how this works. Imagine you want to sell pizzas and need to come up with a good name. You can call your pizza: Pizza, Best Pizza, Alaska's Best Pizza, Suzy's Pizza, A.J.'s Pizza, Mile Pie Pizza, Pizzatastic, Tarantula Pizza, Falling Domino Pizza, or Prazdahada Pizza. Let's take a look at these in order:

1. *Pizza.* This is generic. You can use this name, but anybody else can also use the name and you wont be able to register the name with the USPTO.

2. *Best Pizza, Alaska's Best Pizza, Suzy's Pizza, A.J.'s Pizza.* These are all descriptive names. They merely describe the pizza's quality, geography, or use a personal name or acronym. You most likely will not be able to register any of these names with the USPTO unless you can prove that you've used the name long enough to gain meaning beyond the descriptive name. (McDonald's is a good example.) You might be able to register the name with the state of Alaska. You might also be able to stop someone else from using the name through unfair trade practices laws.

3. *Mile Pie Pizza, Pizzatastic.* These two names are stronger than descriptive names. They are suggestive marks. They use ordinary words in a clever way to create a desirable feeling about the product. They are considered distinctive and therefore protectable. You probably can register these names with the USPTO so long as the name doesn't cause confusion with another protected trademark. But remember, there is no guarantee that the name will be approved.

4. *Tarantula Pizza, Falling Domino Pizza.* These names are arbitrary. You normally don't associate tarantulas or dominos along with pizza. These names use common words used in an unexpected or arbitrary way and are legally strong marks. The USPTO will likely accept the application so long as they don't cause confusion with another protected trademark. The applicant will still need to disclaim rights to the word *Pizza* in the trademark application. The name Falling Domino Pizza, however, is likely too close to the Domino's Pizza trademark and will almost certainly be rejected because it can be easily confused with a protected registered trademark.

5. *Prazdahada Pizza.* I made this name up. Pretty good huh? It's a coined trademark. If this is a brand new word never used before and isn't close to any other name in its class, then the USPTO will almost certainly approve the trademark application.

So let's review the different levels of trademark strength from the weakest to the strongest.

1. *Generic.* These words are synonymous with the underlying product or service and can't be distinguished from others. Names like cola, dry ice, pizza, etc. These names will never receive any protection.

2. *Nondistinctive.* These are ordinary marks. The mark says something about the product or service in a descriptive or otherwise mundane way. These names only receive protection when they become so closely identified with a specific product or service that the public no longer thinks first of the original ordinary meaning of the word (think McDonald's). They also get protection from unfair trade practices laws. Nondistinctive marks include:

- Descriptions. These marks describe a feature or attribute of the product or services such as Best Pet Care, Superb Web Design, etc. It also includes composite words that use fragments such as web-, micro-, compu-, etc.

- Geographic names. These marks include geographic terms like West, Anchorage, Alaska, Denali, world, global or any other place identifier such as street names, regions, rivers, etc.
- Personal names. These include first name, nicknames, surnames, and initials. They're the most popular marks used for goods and services.

Even though non-distinctive marks don't qualify for federal registration, they can be placed on the federal supplemental register. The benefits of doing this are: it gives notice to future trademark searchers; you're allowed to use the ® with the mark; and if the mark remains on the supplemental register for five years it makes it more likely to be placed on the principal register. (All references to federal register in this book refer to the principal register unless otherwise specified.)

3. *Suggestive.* If you use an ordinary word to suggest, but not outright describe an idea or feeling, the mark is considered distinctive and protectable. A good example is Roach Motel.

4. *Fanciful/arbitrary.* If you use ordinary words in an unusual context or create a fanciful association, then the mark is considered distinctive and protectable. A good example is Apple Computer. You won't find any apples in their products. What does an apple have to do with computers? The association is fanciful.

5. *Coined.* These words are made up and mean nothing. They more than likely never existed before. The best example is Kodak. These names receive the most protection.

# *Search*

The first person or company to use or register a distinctive trademark has rights in that mark. If a second person uses a trademark that creates a likelihood of confusion with the first person's trademark, then the second person may have to change the mark and possibly pay damages to the first user. A trademark search helps avoid these problems. It also prevents you from paying fees for rejected applications.

Once you've selected a name, a trademark search looks for the same or similar marks, whether registered or unregistered, to your name. The marks you're looking for are marks used anywhere in the country that are used in a way that might cause confusion. Sometimes these searches are like looking for a needle in a haystack. Other times it's like looking for a steel beam in the haystack.

Fortunately there are many resources to look for those marks that might conflict with the mark you selected. The main sources are:

- federally registered trademarks – www.uspto.gov
- state registered trademark databases
- the internet – domain name searches, Google searches, etc.
- publications – yellow pages, trade publications, other databases

If you get a direct hit in your search, that's great. Your search has been made easy and you've avoided many headaches down the road. But you often don't receive a direct hit. That's where the search becomes an art. You search for homonyms, synonyms, phonetic equivalents, wild cards, truncations, etc. The one thing you can count on is that your search will be incomplete no matter how thorough you are. You just have to live with and accept a small degree of uncertainty.

47

You can always turn to the pros and hire a professional search firm to conduct the search for you. The pros know which databases to search and have mastered the art of searching. Some even have their own proprietary databases. They will not give you legal advice, but they will give you a report of their hits. If you're going to spend a lot of money to create your brand and establish your mark, then it makes sense to pay the pros to conduct the search. It also makes sense to use the pros if you're registering a graphic design.

Generally speaking, if you plan on doing business on the web to a national market, then you should do a more extensive search. If you only plan on using the mark in one state or small region, the less extensive your search needs to be. If you don't have a distinctive name, you should still do a check to avoid a claim of unfair trade practices.

## *Evaluate*

Once you have your search results, you need to determine whether any of the other marks you found would likely create customer confusion between your products or services and their products and services. If confusion is likely, then you should choose another mark (unless you used the mark first, in which case you'll need to deal with the other uses as an infringement). If confusion is unlikely, then you may use the mark.

Unfortunately, this process is not cut and dried. The likelihood of customer confusion is one of those mushy legal terms that depend on the facts. If you ask for an opinion from an attorney, they will likely err on the side of caution. Here are some general guidelines in determining whether there is a likelihood of confusion.

Likelihood means that confusion will more than likely happen; that it's probable. Not that it's already happened or will happen. The second factor is confusion. Will a customer confuse your goods and services with someone else's goods or services? If Apple, Inc. sells computers and Apple Hair Products sells shampoos, it's hard to imagine someone accidentally buying a computer when they meant to buy shampoo.

Here are few things to look at:

- Do the products or services use the same distribution channels?
- Do both products or services appear in the same trade journals?
- Are both products displayed or sold in the same stores?
- Do the products or services target the same customer base?
- Do the products or services sound or look alike?
- Do they cost the same?
- How many customers are confused (is it 5%, 50%, 80%)?
- Does the owner of the mark have a history of infringement lawsuits? (If they do, then move along.)
- Do the marks appear in the same international classification?

# *Register*

You've picked a name, searched for conflicts, and determined that your trademark is distinct and is not likely to cause confusion with any other trademark. Does this mean that you're ready to register it with the USPTO? Not yet. You need to consider whether you need the benefits of federal registration. Remember, you automatically gain trademark rights in all the locations where you use it first. If you market your products to the nation on the internet, this might automatically qualify you for those rights. But even if this is the case, there are advantages to registering your mark with the USPTO.

The benefits of registering your trademark are as follows:

- You gain exclusive nationwide rights to the mark. (Except for those territories where someone used the mark before you did.)
- You get to place the ® symbol after your mark.
- Your trademark appears in the USPTO database for others to see which might thwart would-be infringers.
- You give official notice to everyone that the trademark is unavailable.
- You get to immunize the trademark once five years have elapsed from its registration.
- You stand a greater chance of winning an infringement lawsuit.

If you decide that you want these benefits, then you have to actually use the trademark in commerce. If the mark involves goods, then this means that you've shipped your goods to a store to be sold or sold them in your own store. If the mark is attached to services, it means that you've marketed your services under the trademark and can deliver the services to your customer. If you haven't used the trademark yet in commerce, you may file an intent-to-use application.

If you used the mark in commerce, then it must be used in commerce that Congress regulates. This means you shipped your product across state, territorial, or international boundaries. It also means that you've advertised your services outside your state, used the mark to conducts services across state lines (e-commerce, consulting via phone to out-of-state resident, etc.), or used the mark in services in more than one state, territory, or country. If you haven't used the mark in interstate commerce, but intend to do so, you may file an intent to use application.

Now you're ready to file the application with the USPTO. Before you do, you need to gather some information. It will make the process much easier. You'll need:

- The date you first used the mark in commerce that Congress regulates.
- The party who will own the trademark (you personally or your company).
- A specimen showing how the mark is used:

  For goods: a photo of labels, tags, containers showing the mark (don't use advertising materials, price lists, internal company documents, catalogs, press releases). For services – a scanned copy of brochures, billboards, direct mail pieces, menus, advertising and marketing materials, letterhead stationary and business cards, screenshot of a full web a page (don't use news releases, invoices, packing slips, or documents only showing trade name).

  A graphic file if you're filing a stylized mark (a word in a specific graphic manner) or design mark

- Your international class selection. (The USPTO uses a system of descriptive categories of goods or services to keep track of registered marks. There are 45 classes in all. You can find these on the USPTO website.)

- Your disclaimers. You may disclaim generic or non-distinctive parts of your trademark such as the word pizza.

If you're registering a name combined with an unusual typeface, you should file an application for the unadorned word and another for the adorned name. If money is an object, then register the unadorned name. If you use your name with a graphic image, you should register the name and the name combined with the graphic image. If money is an object, then file the name combined with the graphic image. If the graphic is not distinctive, then register the name by itself.

With this information in hand you're finally ready to register your trademark. You can either do this online or you can file hard copies. It will cost you $325 to file online (you can file an application for $275 with some pre-filled information) and $375 for paper filing for each international class. When you finish the application, you wait.

An examiner will typically contact you within three to six months of filing. If there's a problem with your application, you'll receive an action letter explaining the problem. You often can fix the problem with a phone call to the examiner. When the examiner approves your application, you'll receive a notice of publication. Anyone can oppose your registration for 30 days after your registration (only 3% of marks are opposed). If no one opposes the registration, you'll receive a certificate of registration.

During this process you might get one of three rejection letters:

- Technical rejections such as incorrect applicant name, ambiguous authority, class identification problems (you can normally fix these problems through an amendment).
- Substantive rejections such as a determination that the

mark is generic or merely descriptive or will likely be confused with another mark (a response takes more effort and may require help from an attorney).

- Final rejections are received normally after you've had a chance to respond to the other two rejections.

If you don't want to fight a rejection or if you receive a final rejection, you may always abandon your application or appeal the decision.

# *Protect*

As soon as you start using your trademark whether you've applied for federal registration or not, you should protect it. If your trademark is federally registered, you can do the following to protect your name:

1. Use the ® symbol. You don't have to use it, but it does provide notice to potential infringers and improves your chances of collecting damages and lost profits in court.

2. File Section 8 and 15 Declarations. Between the fifth and sixth year following federal registration you should file these declarations to tell the USPTO that your mark is still in use and that your registration should continue in force. Your mark will then be incontestable which means it makes it more difficult for someone to challenge your mark.

3. File Section 8 Declaration and Section 9 Renewal. Within six months after the tenth anniversary of your registration, file these documents to renew your registration.

4. Police your trademark. If you don't assert your rights, you might inadvertently abandon them. Policing means conducting periodic trademark searches or even hiring third parties to police your mark. If you discover a potential infringer, you may want to take action to protect your rights. Sometimes you're on the other end and someone will make a claim against you that you're infringing their rights.

In either case you'll want to take a rational approach that doesn't escalate the matter beyond a reasonable resolution of the matter. The resolution often depends on who used the name first, who federally registered the name first, whether the goods or services are similar, and whether there is customer confusion.

# *The Internet*

When you register a domain name, it doesn't automatically gain trademark rights. You only acquire trademark rights if your domain name is distinctive through customer awareness and you are the first to use it in commerce. Amazon.com is a good example.

If you've chosen a domain name and it's available, you should probably do a quick trademark search to see if there's a direct hit. If you don't get a hit, you might consider buying it because someone else might beat you to it first. Names don't cost much. If it turns out that it violates someone else's trademark, you can always transfer it to them (but beware of trademark dilution). Then you can do a more thorough search. If you get a hit, you can go back to the drawing board.

If you've found a good name, but someone else has already registered it and is using it as a trademark, then you should move along and choose something else. If they're not using it as a trademark, you can always offer to buy the domain name from them.

If you already established trademark rights and someone has taken the domain name based on your trademark primarily for the purpose of selling it to you, they are a cyber-squatter. You may sue them in federal court or use a procedure through ICANN to force them to transfer the name to you.

One other thing about the internet. If anyone, anywhere can purchase your goods or services through your website, then the trademark on those goods or services is more than likely given national protection. The same is true of a mail order business in a national magazine.

55

# Leases

Finding a Space
Your Team
Negotiations
Timeline
People
Land, Structures, and Stuff
Money
Fairness
Termination
Liability
Disputes

~

Your lease will most likely be your biggest monthly expense besides your employees and yourself. It will also most likely be your longest obligation. Leases can run from one month, to a few years, to longer than a decade. It makes sense then to make sure you do your best to get it right.

But that's not easy considering all the parties involved and the uncertainty of the future. You have landlords, bankers, brokers, attorneys, insurers, property managers, contractors, architects, and business owners. Your business might be wildly successful or go bust (let's hope for success). The economy might change. Disasters can happen. And the list goes on and on.

Yet many business owners just sign the lease given them by the landlord without much consideration to their own interests and their future. They just want to get into a space and start doing business. That's not always a wise course to take.

There are traps for the unwary. The landlord doesn't necessarily set these traps on purpose. The landlord normally gives you what the landlord's lawyer drafted; the same lawyer who advocates for the landlord, so you'll more than likely get a landlord-favored lease. You also need to consider that the lawyer often cuts and pastes old leases together, not completely realizing what's in the lease. This can lead to disastrous results. So it makes sense for all parties to take a step back and negotiate and draft a lease that works for all parties.

# *Finding a Space*

The best time to search for a space is when you don't need it. This gives you a lot of leverage when you negotiate. It's easy to walk away from negotiations if you're not pressured to get into the space. This gives you a lot of leverage in the negotiations, if the landlord is anxious to lease it. Time is your friend.

If you're under pressure, the next best thing is to fall in love with more than one space. Then you can walk away from negotiations if they aren't going your way and revert to another option. The worst thing you can do is find one space, fall in love with it, and be under a time crunch. You won't have much bargaining power under that scenario. You can still walk away, but then you're back to square one.

Of course, the market will play a part in your negotiating strength. Your broker will help give you an idea of what the market is like.

# *Your Team*

You don't have to wait until you need space to assemble your team. It takes time to find the right people to help make you successful. So start putting your team together as soon as you can. You'll probably need the following:

- Broker: to help you find your space
- Banker: to help finance improvements
- Insurance agent: to help you purchase the right insurance
- Architect/Interior Designer: to help you design your space
- Contractor: to construct tenant improvements
- CPA: to help you figure out how much you can afford and the tax consequences of your decision
- Attorney: to help you negotiate your lease

You'll first start working with your broker to help you find your space. You should also start putting some of your team into action. They'll help you figure out what to look for and how much you can afford.

If you need space designed to your needs, you can engage your architect in helping you figure out the design and size of your space and help you figure out what permits you might need. You can talk with your CPA to help you figure out how much you can afford and how long of a lease you might need. If you're going to need financing, you can talk with your banker. You can also require the owner to engage environmental consultants to conduct an environmental assessment (All Appropriate Inquiry) of potentially contaminated property or request a copy of the report if the owner already conducted the AAI. You can also start looking for a contractor.

It's not a bad idea to let your attorney know that you plan on leasing space. Then your attorney can start drafting a lease that's tailored to your needs. The landlord often has her own lease and will want to use it. But if you have negotiating power, you can insist on using your form. The advantage of using your form is that you can start the negotiations with a tenant-favored lease rather than a landlord-favored lease.

Once you've found a space, you may consider writing a letter of intent stating your terms. Once the letter of intent is signed, it's time to start negotiating the lease.

# *Negotiations*

When all parties sign the letter of intent, you're ready to start negotiating the lease. Sometimes you'll just go straight to the lease without signing a letter of intent. The most important thing to remember is that time is your best friend. What's an extra month when you're signing a ten-year lease? The longer you have to negotiate, the better your lease will be.

There are a few things you should do before you sign the lease. Hopefully you've already engaged your attorney in the negotiations. Don't give a copy of the lease to the attorney to review at the last moment. You've lost a lot of your bargaining power by that point. It's also a good idea to have your insurance agent read the whole lease and make sure that you have the right policies in place. You should consider investigating the landlord. You can ask for references and talk to other tenants. A good lease with a bad landlord doesn't make a good combination. You might consider getting a title report to make sure that your intended use doesn't violate any land use restrictions. You might want to make a list of contractors for landord approval.

Now we're finally ready to start talking about the actual lease. Everything we've talked about so far helps assure that you'll get a good lease. It will help you make good decisions when you're negotiating the actual provisions of the lease.

When we talk about your lease, we're talking about your future. All a lease can do is cover items that typically happen in a landlord/tenant relationship and the things that are less likely to happen, but are better handled in a lease rather than when the event happens. The lease is also a valuable tool to establish expectations among all the parties. That's why it's a good idea to spend a couple of hours with all parties before signing the lease to go over each provision.

Once you sign your lease, you're bound by its terms. We'll look at a typical life of a lease, the parties, money, fairness, and changes—all to help you better understand the terms of a typical lease.

# *Timeline*

Your lease specifies how events will unfold—from making improvements, to moving in, to making repairs, to doing maintenance, to renewing and exercising options, to terminating the lease, and finally to moving out.

Hopefully you already have things in motion when you sign the lease. If you plan on making improvements to the space, the landlord will often give you a tenant improvement allowance. You'll want to get going on these improvements as soon as possible. This means having permits in place, drawings and specifications, contractors, financing, etc.

When the tenant improvements are done, it's time to move in. Or, if your lease doesn't involve improvements, you'll move in on the date specified in the lease. When the landlord delivers the premises to you, inspect the premises to make sure you get what's in your lease.

Then you use the space for the term of the lease. Time will take it's toll on the property—it will need maintenance; it will need repairs or improvements; and as time goes on the space might need to be altered for your expanding or contracting business. Some of these items will be minor and some will be structural. Some will be caused by nature, the landlord, or other parties. Some will be caused by you. These items might cause minor disruptions to your business or major disruptions, even temporary closure. They will all cost money. They will also require inspections of your leased space.

A few things you may want to consider including in your lease are an option to expand your space or an allowance for refurbishment for longer leases. You can always ask the landlord for an option to extend the lease. If you're interested in buying the property, you can ask for an option to buy the property or the right of first refusal.

Then the lease ends. You return the property in good condition. Make sure that you don't get stuck with the responsibility to remove your alterations or improvements. Otherwise, budget for them. The landlord gives you your security deposit back. And you move on. The lease and the relationship is done.

# *People*

Even though a lease is between a landlord and tenant, there are others who are not part of the lease but have a connection with the landlord and tenant. They might have obligations such as maintenance or improvements. Let's take a look at them.

## The Landlord's Owners

These are the owners of the landlord if its an entity such as an LLC. They more than likely formed an LLC to protect their personal assets. This means that the LLC is often highly leveraged and doesn't have many assets. If the landlord is an LLC or corporation and is funding your tenant improvements, you may want to get a guarantee from their owners.

## The Tenant's Owners

These are the owners of the tenant if it's an entity such as an LLC. The landlord wants to make sure that it will get its money. Often the tenant is either heavily leveraged or thin on assets. The landlord often requires the tenant's owners to sign personal guarantees. This exposes their homes, savings, cars, and other personal assets to liability for everything that's in the lease. The tenant should try to make sure that the guarantee terminates if the tenant transfers the lease to another party, or the tenant should try to get more time to make payments and limit the affects of rent acceleration on the personal guarantee.

## Bankers

The landlord often finances the space you're leasing with a loan from the bank. The bank secures the loan with the property.

The bank might want you to confirm that your lease is enforceable and that there are no uncured defaults. The bank will want you to subordinate your interest in your lease to the bank's interest. They'll want you to acknowledge any new landlord that takes over the property after a loan default or foreclosure. You'll want to make sure that none of your lease rights are affected by the landlord's relationship with the bank.

## Insurers

Besides rent, your biggest liability exposure is for property damage and any injuries that happen on your leased space, the common areas, parking, etc. There is also exposure for environmental issues such as hazardous waste. If someone is injured, property is damaged, or environmental liability is incurred, your insurance and the landlord's insurance should kick into gear.

Most leases include clauses that try to push the landlord's liability to your insurer. There are waivers of subrogation, additional insured provisions, and primary insured requirements. You'll want to make sure that liability is divided appropriately between you and the landlord. This includes mutual waivers of subrogation, mutual additional insured provisions, and no primary insured provisions.

## Property Managers

The property manager takes care of the operations and maintenance of the leased space. You can set their duties and standards in the lease.

## Brokers

The tenant or landlord or both may have brokers or negotiate on their own. These brokers can receive hefty fees. Make sure you know who will pay their fees and how much they will be involved in the management of the lease.

## Contractors

Some contractors are better than others. Some do better work then others. The work often takes longer than anticipated and they will need to be paid. You'll need to determine how much control you want over the contractors and their progress. When the lease is done the question of who owns the improvements comes into play.

## Competitors

What happens if your landlord leases a nearby space to one of your competitors? It could damage your business. This is something to consider if you know your landlord has other property to lease. You might want to get exclusive rights to operate your business in an industry or location.

## Sublessors and Assigns

You might outgrow your space or need to move to a smaller space. No matter what you do, you're on the hook for the total term of the lease. So you might want to sublease your space or even assign it. These are two very different things and you'll want to make sure you have certain rights with each. For example, you may want to ask the landlord for a total release from your obligations if you transfer the lease to someone else.

## Clients and Customers

You may have hundreds, even thousands of customers come and go from your space during the life of your lease. Hopefully they will come and go without mishap. But slips and falls happen. What if it happens in your space? What if it happens in a common area? What if the landlord's faulty maintenance causes it? The insurance and liability provisions need to divide liability for these accidents between you and the landlord.

## Government

Sometimes the government will take an interest in your space. Whether its through inspections, eminent domain, or other laws, you'll want to cover what happens when the government gets involved in your lease.

## Landlord and Tenant

This is the main relationship of the whole lease. The key item is rent, but also includes security deposits, defaults and accelerations. The lease provides a valuable opportunity to set expectations between the parties and to discuss up front what happens if the lease doesn't work out.

## Co-tenants

How will co-tenants use their space? You don't want a bar next to a childcare center. You may rely on an anchor tenant. What happens if the anchor tenant moves or closes its doors? You should monitor co-tenants to protect co-tenancy rights and require co-tenants to be open for business when you open for business.

# Land, Structures, and Stuff

## Your Space

It sounds simple enough to identify the space you're leasing. But does it include hallways, bathrooms, workrooms, etc.? In order to avoid confusion, it's best to include a drawing of the leased space and attach it as an exhibit. You might want to get an aerial photograph of the area. If you're paying by square footage, you'll want to get measurements.

## Common Areas

These are the areas that all tenants and guests can use. You'll want to include these on the map talked about above. Then you and the landlord need to agree on who is responsible for maintaining these areas and the extent of the maintenance. If you're sharing these costs with the landlord and other tenants, make sure you understand the formula and that the formula is worked into your budget.

## Parking

You'll want plenty of parking for you, your employees, and customers. This is another item to include on your map.

## Signs

You want people to see your business. Your signs play an important part in your marketing effort. Find out if there are limitations on size, color, location, etc. If there aren't any limitations, you should decide what sort of sign you want, then make sure you include the specifications in the lease.

## Fixtures

These are things you add to the lease, but don't become a part of the structure. At the end of the lease it's easy to have misunderstandings about what stays with the structure and what you can take with you. If you make alterations, improvements, or repairs, you might want to take some of these with you when the lease ends. This requires you to alter the structure. Figure out how you want to handle this at the end of the lease.

## The Land

Your lease sits on land. Sometimes you'll store items on the land. If you suspect that the land has environmental issues (such as with a gas station or warehouse), then consider getting an environmental assessment of the land from an environmental consulting firm. Then you'll have a benchmark on the property. If you don't suspect that hazardous activity occurred on the property, still get a warranty from the landlord that the land is free from such activity.

## Structures

Your lease includes much you don't see: wiring, plumbing, roof, sidewalks, HVAC, grease traps, etc. You don't notice these things when they're running right, but if something goes wrong, you'll know it soon enough. Faulty plumbing can cause a mess for you and your business. A leak in the roof can be miserable. When these things happen it's good to know who is responsible to make things right, who will pay for it, and how long it will take.

## Services

Along with structural items there are the main services you need to operate your business: electricity, elevators, heat, water, HVAC, wi-fi, phone, IT, janitorial services, snow removal, etc. You want these services uninterrupted. If for some reason they're interrupted, your lease can specify who's responsible to get them back up running, how fast they need to do it, and who's going to pay for it.

## Use

You operate certain services or you create products. Clients and customers come to your space. Sometimes you sell things. Whatever you do, make sure that your lease allows you to do it in all the locations you need to do it.

# *Money*

This seems like a simple matter, but money can get complicated. Let's break down each piece.

## Tenant Improvements

If your landlord gives you a tenant improvement allowance, you should decide how and when it will be paid, what it includes (including soft costs such as architectural fees, legal fees, building permit fees, signage costs, moving costs, etc.), and what happens if the landlord fails to pay you back for reimbursable costs. You may want to require the landlord to place the money in escrow.

## Rent Calculation

Rent can be as easy as paying a flat amount monthly for everything you need to operate in your space. It can also include complicated formulas broken into parts. Here are some items that might be included in your rent:

- Property taxes: address special assessments in this item.
- Insurance: find out about premiums and what happens when prices increase.
- Common Areas Maintenance: this is often shared between the landlord and other tenants; but the wrong formula can be costly.
- Utilities: make a detailed list of who pays what. If the landlord pays utilities, make sure that it's not a profit center for them.
- Capital expenses: do you have to pay for any capital expenses? If so, how and when?

If any part of your rent is based on a formula, then get the right to audit and review the books and records and to reconcile statements.

## Rent Abatement

The ability to abate your rent based on defaults is one of the most powerful ways to force your landlord to comply with the lease. Otherwise you have to take them to court and get an order, which can take a long time.

# *Fairness*

If your landlord provides you with a lease, more than likely it will be one-sided. You often can correct the imbalance by requiring reciprocal provisions. The following are the most common types of clauses that should be reciprocal:

- Indemnification. The landlord typically tries to push all risk and liability to the tenant. The tenant should push some of this risk and liability back to the landlord.
- Force Majeure. The landlord typically tries to push the risks of unforeseen events such as earthquakes, fires, etc. to the tenant. The tenant should push back some of these risks to the landlord.
- Hazardous Materials. Require the landlord to provide you with an environmental warranty promising that the space isn't contaminated. Also require the landlord to defend and indemnify you if the warranty is breached. Require the landlord to pay cleanup costs. Ask for the right for rent abatement and the right to terminate the lease if hazardous waste interrupts your business. You may also require environmental insurance.
- Insurance and Waivers of Subrogation. The landlord typically tries to push their risk to the tenant's insurance. The tenant should push these risks back onto the landlord's insurance.
- Waiver of Claims. The landlord might try to require the tenant to waive claims against the landlord without a reciprocal waiver. If the landlord wants waivers from the tenant, the tenant should ask for waivers from the landlord.

- Default clause. Include a provision that specifies landlord defaults such as the landlord's failure to pay for tenant improvements, the failure to comply with the lease terms and obligations, and any representations and warranties that prove to be false.
- Remedies. Include your remedies such as lost profits, relocation expenses, attorney's fees, punitive damages, recission for failure to deliver, injunctions, specific performance to perform required act, and declaratory judgment to declare who is right.
- Damage and Destruction. The landlord often requires the tenant to pay for damage and destruction the tenant causes without a reciprocal responsibility. The tenant should require the landlord to pay for damage and destruction it causes.

# *Termination*

Most of the time you'll stay in your space until the lease ends. But what happens when your business doesn't work out? You're still on the hook for the entire term of the lease. If you default, then the landlord can more than likely terminate the lease and accelerate the total amount of the remaining rent. So it's hardly ever a good idea to vacate the lease. But you can include some clauses that will soften the blow. And you can always try to renegotiate the lease.

## Sublease or Assignment

You can find someone to take over your lease. If you sublease, it's as if you're still renting the place in the eyes of the owner. Your sublease is just between you and the sublessor. You're still on the hook for rent and everything else. However, if you assign the lease, then you step back and the party to whom you assigned the lease works directly with the landlord.

## Gross Sales Trigger

You can try to negotiate a provision that allows you to terminate the lease if your gross sales fall below a certain number.

## Option to Reduce Space

You can try to negotiate an option that allows you to reduce the rented space at a later date.

## Going Dark

You can try to negotiate the right to go dark. If it makes more sense for you to shut down your business, then a go dark right allows you to close the doors without triggering a default in your lease. Then you can pay the monthly rent and look for someone to sublease or assign your lease. You'll want to consider preventing an anchor tenant from going dark.

## Key Person

If a key person in your business dies, then your estate might be stuck with the lease obligation without a viable business to maintain the lease. You can ask the landlord to agree to terminate the lease if a key person dies.

If an anchor tenant moves or goes dark, then you may want to consider asking for the right to reduce rent or terminate the lease until the landlord finds a suitable replacement that brings in the right type of customer.

# *Liability*

We've already talked about this, but it needs some more discussion. If someone is injured and the injury is related to your lease or if there is property damage, then the lease plays a key role in deciding who pays. You and your landlord should have insurance to cover these claims, but these sorts of things still take a lot of your time. They also cause a lot of anxiety. So you'll want to minimize this as much as possible.

The lease will normally specify how liability should be divided between the parties. If it doesn't, then the law will decide liability.

One way to divide liability is to base it on the percentage that each party is at fault. But this requires lots of litigation.

Another way to do this is to base liability on parties and property regardless of fault. Each party takes care of their property, contractors, and employees. This lessens intensive fact-based fights. There are a few other things to consider in this arrangement such as worker's comp claims. You also need to make sure that each of you purchases insurance to cover your liability and each party is named as an additional insured on each other's policies if someone tries to tag you for something that the other person has assumed liability for. That way your defense costs can be covered. Then if a third-party is injured, the landlord and tenant are liable for the injury to the extent of their fault.

# *Disputes*

Everyone starts out happy, but life unfolds, events play on us, and relationships can go sour. It's good to have a mechanism in your lease for resolving disputes. The best way to avoid disputes is to communicate. If everyone understands each other's expectations and is informed of changes, then matters can be dealt with before they explode into larger problems.

If a dispute can't be resolved, then it's a good practice to require the parties to mediate their disputes. If mediation doesn't work, then the parties have two options: they can arbitrate or they can go to court. There were high hopes for arbitration, but it has turned out to be just as onerous as litigation in some cases. It's also expensive. The parties pay for the arbitrator's time which can be hundreds of dollars per hour, then you're stuck with the arbitrator's decision. You can't appeal it. Some have said that arbitrators often just split the baby. Yet, it's still quicker than litigation.

Litigation on the other hand takes a lot of time. The judges are busy and have many other cases. But the rules are more defined; you can appeal a decision and you don't have to pay for the judge's time. In Alaska there are loser pay rules and offers of judgment that help bring cases to settlement. You can ask for a settlement conference with the judge. And you can agree to waive your right to a jury trial which speeds up the process, but leaves you at the mercy of the judge.

So take these into consideration and choose your dispute resolution procedures appropriately.

# Employees

Independent Contractor
Discrimination
Privacy
An Employee Handbook
Health and Safety
Hiring
Documents
Evaluations
Wages
Terminations
References
Miscellaneous

~

You need employees to get things done. But when you hire employees, you also hire risk. Here are 10 general rules to minimize employee risks:

1. Set clear expectations between you and your employees in a concise and well-written employee handbook.
2. Base all employment decisions on relevant and legal factors.
3. Encourage coworkers to live the golden rule.
4. Keep the job-site safe.
5. Document and date things as they happen and get signatures. But don't go crazy with documentation.
6. Don't be a jerk. Hostile, intimidating, and offensive behavior has no place in the workplace.
7. Look into employment practices liability insurance.
8. Be consistent in training, reviews, and enforcement.
9. Read lots of business books.
10. Respect your employees' reasonable expectations of privacy.

If you follow these rules, you will go a long way toward avoiding costly and time-consuming legal disputes.

# *Independent Contractors*

You can't do it all on your own. You'll probably hire outside people to do a lot of work for you. This works out great, you don't have to pay employment taxes, workers' compensation, unemployment compensation, benefits, and office space and equipment for these people. You don't have to worry about wage and hour law, family and medical leave, and many other laws that apply to your employees. You're not liable for their negligence (unless they're acting as your agent), and they can't make worker's comp claims against you (though they can make claims for your negligence).

But your business starts to grow. Maybe you need someone on the weekend to stock shelves. Maybe you need someone to help you write a proposal. You buy equipment for them to do their job. You give them space in your office. You start needing them more and more. This is where it gets dangerous. If you start to control what is to be done and how it's done, then your independent contractor might now be your employee. Once they are your employee, you're required to pay things such as payroll taxes and worker's comp and you're now subject to many employment laws. It's a whole new world.

There's no clear line when this happens, each law or agency has it's own factors to determine where that line is. The DOL has its own, the IRS has its own, and there's also case law for tort liability. But all of them have similar factors.

If you ask yourself the following questions, you'll more than likely be safe with all these laws and agencies:
- Do you provide instruction to the person?
- Do you provide training to the person?

- Does this person use your trademarks?
- Do you invest in equipment and other items to support the individual?
- Do you reimburse the person for business expenses?
- Is the person prohibited from pursuing other business or employment opportunities?
- Is the person prevented from earning a profit or loss from the work?
- Does the person work without a written contract?
- Does the person perform key aspects of your business?

The more yes answers means the person is more than likely your employee and not an independent contractor.

What happens if you get it wrong? You must pay for the person's social security tax, federal income tax, and unemployment insurance for three years plus interest and penalties. You might be liable for overtime wages and penalties. There might be ramifications for workers' compensation and other laws that apply to employees. You might be liable for their negligence.

The best way to avoid a misclassification is to sign contracts with your independent contractors. You get much more protection if the contract is with a corporation or a limited liability company.

# *Discrimination*

There are some things that always need to be in the forefront of your mind whenever you're preparing job descriptions, writing ads, conducting interviews, deciding whom to hire, setting salaries and job benefits, promoting employees, and disciplining and firing employees.

The first thing to remember is that you may not indirectly or directly discriminate against anyone based on the following:

- Race
- Color
- Religion
- Sex: this includes pregnancy and sexual harassment such as unwelcome sexual advances, requests for sexual favors, and other verbal or physical conduct of a sexual nature that creates a hostile or abusive work environment.
- National origin: if you have four or more employees, the law requires you to treat those who have been lawfully admitted to the United States the same as all other employees.
- Disability: if you have 15 or more employees, the law prohibits you from discriminating against anyone because of disability. This means that you may need to buy special equipment, eliminate non-essential duties, and make reasonable accommodations. You may not ask medical questions or require a medical exam before a job offer is made. Once the offer is made you may require a medical exam. If the exam reveals a disqualifying condition, then you may withdraw the job offer.

- Age: if you have 20 or more employees, the law prohibits you from discriminating against anyone who is 40 years old or older.

You are under a duty to take steps to prevent discrimination by providing anti-discrimination policies, promptly investigating complaints, and disciplining employees who have unlawfully discriminated against other employees.

If you illegally discriminate against or retaliate against one of your employees, you may have to rehire, promote, or reassign them; compensate them for lost salary and benefits; pay damages for emotional suffering; change your policies; and pay the employee's legal fees.

# *Privacy*

Every employee has a reasonable expectation of privacy when they use the phone, send an email, use the internet, store personal belongings at work, etc. But employers have the right to take measures to detect theft, thwart the disclosure of confidential information, and prevent discrimination.

The resolution between these competing interest is that if you tell your employees that you plan to monitor their activities during work, they no longer have a reasonable expectation of privacy. You may give this notice in the employee handbook or through posted notices. If you get written consent from your employees acknowledging your policy, that's even better.

But there are limits. You should have a business necessity when you monitor your employees or conduct a search. If you come across something that is personal and non-work related, then stop reading it or monitoring it. Be careful in how you limit off-duty activities such as office romances, but be wary of romances between a supervisor and subordinate. Be consistent in any disciplinary action. Never search your employee's person. Call the police to conduct such a search. Limit your searches to company-owned property and try not to search the employee's personal property.

# An Employee Handbook

Your employee handbook is the main tool for setting expectations between you and your employees. It also helps avoids misunderstanding. You don't have to have one, but if you don't, it's easy to be inconsistent and rely on verbal communications which can expose you to legal disputes.

You should implement procedures to make sure every employee receives a copy and acknowledges receiving the employee handbook and reading it. Make sure you follow it and beware of statements that modify your right to terminate your employees without cause (at-will employment).

Keep your handbook simple. Make sure it includes at-will language and a description of the procedure for employment contracts. Reserve your right to terminate an employee without cause.

The handbook should include items such as hours, pay, benefits including paid vacations, health benefits, sick pay, unpaid leave; whether vacation days can be carried into next year; and what happens when an employee quits. It should also include policies on things such as discrimination and sexual harassment, drug and alcohol abuse, social media, and safety. It should include your disciplinary procedures.

Your handbook should also include reporting mechanisms, investigation procedures, and disciplinary measures such as warnings, suspensions, transfers, demotions, and terminations. It should include non-retaliation standards. You might consider having a code of conduct. If you're a government contractor, the law might require you to have a compliance and ethics program in place.

# Health and Safety

It goes without saying that safety is important. But I'll go ahead and say it: "Safety is critical to your business." It saves you money, saves you time, makes for happier employees, and it will keep the government out of your hair. So have some sort of safety code in place and do your best to make sure your employees follow it.

The main law is OSHA. If you just have one employee, then it applies to you. It's a big law with a hefty load of regulations, and you must enact procedures, train employees, post notices, enforce violations, and discipline employees. If you have ten or more employees and are not in the retail trade, real estate, insurance, financial business, or service business (all with some exceptions), then you have reporting requirements. If you violate OSHA, they can levy serious fines on you.

OSHA inspectors can inspect your workplace without notice or a court order, unless you have a workplace with ten or fewer employees in an industry with a low injury rate. If you're a small business, OSHA more than likely will not inspect you unless one of your employees has made a complaint to OSHA, a worker has died at the workplace, or three or more employees are hospitalized because of a workplace condition. You can refuse to let OSHA in for an inspection without a court order, but that just makes them mad. You can always ask for an extension of time to talk with your lawyer.

If you have an employee, then you must get workers' compensation insurance. Here's how it works. Worker's comp is a no-fault system. If your employee is injured while at work, it doesn't matter who's at fault (unless you intentionally caused the injury), they get worker's comp. But your liability is limited by law to partial wage replacement and payment of medical bills. Your insurer covers these costs which means you're only liable for premiums and any amounts not covered by your insurer. The premium is based on your industry and payroll.

Another big area is drug and alcohol abuse. You may combat alcohol and illegal drug use in the workplace; you don't need to tolerate absenteeism, tardiness, poor job performance, or accidents caused by substance abuse; but you must have a written program in place if you want to require drug testing. The program should cover pre-employment testing, post employment testing, and other testing standards. Alcoholism is subject to the ADA.

If someone is injured on the job, then seek medical attention right away, then complete an accident report, file a worker's comp claim, report the accident to OSHA, and consider disciplinary action on the employees who contributed to causing the accident.

If you designate a smoking area, it must be ventilated so that non-smokers aren't subject to second-hand smoke.

# *Hiring*

Your business is growing and you need help. That's the good news. But now you need to hire someone. You'll need to write a job description, advertise, get applications, interview, decide whether to hire, make the offer, and complete the intake of the new employee.

For larger companies this process can be long and involved. For small employers, all of this can take place within hours. But no matter how long the process, you still need to follow the law. There should be no discrimination at any point during each step and you must respect the applicant's privacy.

Here are some red flags to watch out for: if a man is hired instead of a woman, a white applicant instead of a minority, a younger worker instead of an older worker, a non-disabled person instead of a disabled person, an American instead of someone of a different national origin.

## Job Descriptions
It's good to write a job description so that you focus on what it takes to get the job done. The description should include safety requirements, qualifications such as skills, education, experience, or licenses, essential job functions, and non-essential functions.

## Advertise
If you advertise for the job don't use gender words like *-man, gal, -tress*, words that reveal age such as *student, young*, and words that might discourage protected classes from applying.

## Applications

In your application ask only for job-related information such as educational background, employment history, special training or achievements related to the job, the date they can start work, etc.

Don't ask for non-job related stuff such as age, birthdate, height or weight, gender (Mrs., Mr.), marital status (single, married, number of children), national origin (lineage, ancestry), arrests that didn't result in conviction, organizations (clubs, societies), personal finance, and photographs.

## Interviews

When you interview the applicant stick to job-related stuff.

## Testing

A lie detector test may not be used in Alaska as a condition of employment (there are a few exceptions such as the hiring of police officers). You can require skill testing if the skills you're testing are related to the job. It's best to stay away from aptitude and psychological tests. Your testing requirements must apply to all entering employees who do the same job. You may withdraw an offer based on results if the reasons are job-related or to avoid a direct threat to health and safety, and you are unable to make reasonable accommodations.

In order to do drug testing in Alaska the employer must have a written policy; the employees must be informed of the policy and provided with a copy; and prospective employees must be informed.

## Investigations

If you need driving records, criminal histories, credit reports, employment reference checking, or school transcripts, you must give notice of the requirement to the applicant, get their consent, and provide a copy of the consent to the person with the information. You must also make sure that there is a business need for the information. Be careful searching the internet for information about an applicant. You may discover unlawful information that can come back and bite you.

## Job Offers

When you make the offer, make sure that you don't make promises of job security and the like. Draft an offer letter so that there's no confusion about the job title, starting date, benefits, and salary. You should also refer to your employee handbook, disclaim oral commitments, and remind the new employee about their at-will status and how it can be altered.

Sometimes, someone will want an employment contract such as an experienced executive, someone leaving a secure job, someone who moves far away, or a person with a particular skill. The contract should include incentives, reasons for terminating the relationship, severance pay, etc.

It's a good idea to send a short letter to rejected applicants.

# *Documents*

If you're ever sued for an employment case, the first thing the attorney will ask for are the employee handbook and the employee's employment file. So it's smart to have well-written policies and a good paper trail. When you document items, don't back date, don't over-document, document the events as they occur, date all documents, sign all documents, get the employee's signature, and inform the employee that the document will go into their personnel file.

The documents that should be in every employment file are: the job description, a completed job application, the offer letter, an acknowledgment of receiving and reading the employee handbook, confidentiality and non-compete agreements, form I-9, W-4s, new-hire reporting, employee benefits, performance evaluations, customer and coworker complaints, awards, warnings and disciplinary action, attendance or tardiness records, etc. You should let the employee add to their file and review it periodically

If there are mistakes, make sure to correct them. Keep the employment file confidential. Allow your employees to access their file with supervision and inform your employees when you add something to their file.

Finally, make sure you comply with government reporting requirements and keep records of the reports.

# *Evaluations*

It's not clear whether evaluations improve performance or safety. But it does provide you with a good system to document performance. If you conduct evaluations, tell it like it is. If something's not good, give examples, set goals, and follow up. Warn the employee that failure to improve might lead to disciplinary action. These need to be systematic and ongoing. Don't be excessively lenient, don't avoid the ends of the rating scale, and base it on the whole evaluation period.

# *Wages*

You may pay most executive, administrative, and professional employees a salary. You may also pay highly paid employees, outside sales employees, computer systems analysts and programmers a salary. These employees have high-level management duties, autonomy, supervise others, make important business decisions, and have a fair amount of authority.

You must pay everyone else by the hour. These are employees who make things and serve the customers. If these employees work more than eight hours a day or more than forty hours per week, you must pay them overtime wages.

If you pay someone a salary when you should have paid them by the hour, you may be subject to an overtime claim. You might have to pay liquidated damages (double unpaid overtime), unless you acted in good faith and reasonably believed there was no wage violation. You can limit your risk by getting DOL approval of your classification or an opinion from legal counsel.

You must pay all nonexempt employees at least a minimum wage. You're required to post certain notices regarding pay. You must pay equal pay and benefits to men and women who do the same or equivalent work. There are laws for tips and commission. You don't have to pay for commuting time, meal and rest breaks (if employees are relieved from all duties), or on-call time controlled by the employee for their own enjoyment or benefit.

Make sure you follow payroll tax rules for withholding taxes, cost of meals, housing, transportation, loans, child support, alimony, insurance premiums, debts and wage garnishments, etc.

# *Terminations*

If an employee doesn't have a written contract (this is different from an offer letter), then the employee is *at will.* This means the employee can quit for no reason at all or whatever reason he or she wants. The employer can fire the employee for no reason or whatever reason he or she wants, except for the following areas which are a basis for a wrongful discharge claim:

- Illegal reasons such as discrimination
- Public policy violations including retaliation against an employee who refused to do something illegal, who exercised their legal rights such as voting, or who blew the whistle
- Oral promises such as a promise of job security
- Breach of the covenant of good faith and fair dealing such as firing someone right before their retirement vests

You should have a well thought out, documented, and legitimate business reason for terminating an employee to protect yourself against a wrongful discharge claim. You're typically free to lay off an employee if your business requires a reduction in force (there are special requirements for employers with more than 100 employees). Other lawful reasons include poor performance, insubordination, excessive absences, dishonesty, criminal activity, using drugs or alcohol at work, disclosing trade secrets, etc.

Before you terminate your employee, you should make sure you haven't made any oral promises of longevity, you don't have a written contract with the employee stating an employment term, or provisions in your employee handbook making promises of job security. You should also make sure there isn't a whiff of discrimination or any other illegal reason in the decision. You should also check your employee handbook to make sure you follow procedures.

If the decision is based on an allegation such as sexual harassment, make sure that the decision to terminate is based on a well-documented and complete investigation with factual conclusions. You may also consider alternatives to termination such as reassignment, counseling, allowing the employee to look for a new job during work hours, etc.

You may want to consider offering a severance package to your employee. You don't have to give a severance unless you agreed to provide severance in an employment contract or employee handbook. Normally the severance is commensurate with the duration of employment. You should make the severance conditional on the employee signing a release of all legal claims. There are special requirements for releases signed by employees who are 40 years old or older. You may also consider allowing the employee to resign, offer to make a favorable reference, or help the employee find a new job.

Before the termination meeting make a list of all the company property that the employee is to return. You may also want to enlist IT to make sure that the employee doesn't delete or take emails and other electronic data. This should be done consistent with your policies.

Meet with the employee in private with another manager. State the reasons for termination, explain the benefits and severance, if any, and let the employee respond. Then just listen. Don't argue. Allow a day or two to clear out belongings and to say goodbye, unless the employee is likely to be a menace. You may include a termination letter and provide it to the employee at this meeting. You may also want to remind the employee about their confidentiality and non-compete obligations. Make sure that you give the employee the final paycheck, benefits, and provide a COBRA notice. You must pay the final paycheck within three days if you terminate the employee or at the next regular pay day if the employee quits.

# *References*

After the employee is terminated you might receive inquiries about the employee from other businesses. Be careful how you respond; otherwise you might find yourself in a defamation claim. The only way they can prove such a claim is to prove that you knew that the information you offered was false, but you passed it along anyway or that you were reckless in sorting out the facts.

You may take the most cautious approach and don't tell them anything. You may limit your response to a confirmation that the employee worked for you and provide the dates the employee worked for you. You may provide the facts in good faith, but be careful when you do. As soon as you start getting into speculation or rumor, you're in dangerous territory. If your motivation in providing the facts is to hurt the ex-employee or cover up the truth, you're also in dangerous territory. It's also tough to know how to word things when the employee has both positives and negatives. So the best policy is: if you're going to give facts, only give them when you have good things to say; otherwise just provide the name, position, and term of the employee when there's something negative.

# *Miscellaneous*

## Covenant of Good Faith and Fair Dealing

Every employer/employee relationship is governed by the covenant of good faith and fair dealing. This means you must treat similar employees the same, you may not terminate an employee for unconstitutional reasons or in violation of public policy, and you can't deprive an employee of a contract benefit.

## Unions

This section doesn't cover unions. If you have employees who want to unionize, you should contact your attorney to figure out your response.

## Benefits

Employee benefits such as health care, disability, retirement, life insurance, educational assistance, dependent care, etc. is a broad topic requiring expertise from your financial planner. Generally you don't have to provide any benefits to your employees (health care reform may bring some changes to larger employers). However, if you offer benefits, make sure you offer them equally to all employees and that you follow reporting, notice and plan requirements to get the proper tax credits and deductions. If you have 20 or more employees and offer group coverage, then COBRA applies to you. There are many other laws that apply to these benefits. Be careful what you say in your employee handbook about benefit obligations. Don't lock yourself in; otherwise you might make yourself a self-insurer.

## Family Medical and Leave Act

If you have 50 or more employees, the law might require you to provide employees with up to 12 weeks of unpaid leave for certain family and medical reasons. You must return that employee to the same or similar position once the leave period is over.

## Taxes

Employment taxes is a broad topic. You should contact your CPA with your employment tax questions.

## Minors

Alaska Laws for minors under the of age 18 provide that the minor may not work more than six days a week, may not work in hazardous occupations, and must get 30 minute breaks. If the child is under the age of 16, the child may not work more than a combined nine hour day which includes their time at school and no more than 23 hours a week. Babysitting and domestic work are exceptions.

# Buy-Sell Agreements

Right of First Refusal
Texas Shoot-Out
Forced Sales
Funding
Price
Ownership

A buy-sell agreement is like a pre-nuptial for your business. If you have a partner, then you should have one. If you're on your own, own the business with your spouse, or plan on leaving the business to your children, then you probably don't need one.

Here's how it works: All of the owners decide which events trigger a right or option to purchase each other's interest in the business. The owners then decide how to determine the price and payment terms when that event is triggered.

So why should you do this? Let's look at the Beatles. Let's say Ringo dies, divorces, is disabled, wants out, or anything else that changes ownership in the band. If one of these events happened the band might end up with a new drummer they don't want. They can offer to buy Ringo's interest in the band, but they might not have the money to do this. All of this can end up in some nasty and expensive disputes.

It's best to avoid such disputes by deciding these issues when everyone is happy—during the honeymoon period. That makes things much easier, creates a market for the business interest (because often it's difficult to sell less than 100% interest to an outsider), and keeps ownership stable. Even the Beatles split up.

# *Right of First Refusal*

There might come a day when an owner wants out of the business. There are a few ways to handle this.

The first way is an outright prohibition of a transfer. This is harsh and hardly ever used. Another way is to require the consent of the other owners before an owner sells his interest. But this gives a lot of power to the consenting owners who can force down the price. Another way to handle this is to prohibit a sale except to qualified buyers or certain individuals. None of these options work every well.

The better way is for owners to agree that the company and all of the owners have a right of first refusal on any offer from an outsider to purchase an owner's interest in the company. Here's how it works.

An owner places his or her own interest up for sale and gets a bona fide offer. The selling owner must give the other owners a detailed notice of the offer (this might include a copy of the offer itself). The company or other owners then have so many days to exercise their option to buy the interest under the terms in the offer. If the company and other owners don't exercise their option, then the selling owner is free to sell the owner's interest to the original outside buyer. This is a balanced approach that allows owners to sell their interest for a good price while allowing the remaining owners to retain some control over new members.

# Texas Shootout

When members have equal voting rights, they can be dead-locked on a decision. This can severely hinder the progress of the business. Most of the time owners can work together and find a solution, but when they can't they'll need some sort of mechanism to break the deadlock.

There's no real clean solution to a deadlock. The least of all evils is a texas shootout provision. Here's how it works.

When owners are deadlocked, any owner may offer to buy-out another owner's interest. The owner that receives the offer has two choices: buy the interest for the price in the offer or force a sale of his own interest on the owner that made the first offer at the same price. One member gets to cut the cake and the other owner gets to choose the piece. This keeps the business together and allows an owner to walk away.

# *Forced Sales*

Sometimes events such as death, disability, a lost license, and early retirement change things. The owners and the company can respond to these changes by creating a right, but not the obligation, to force a buyout of the deceased owner's estate, the disabled owner, the owner whose license was suspended or revoked, or the retired owner.

## Death

When an owner dies, the owner's spouse, children, or whomever else is the beneficiary of their interest becomes the new owner. The remaining owners may not want to be in business with this new owner. In that case, the remaining owners and the company will want to have the option to purchase the new owner's interest. This should be an all or nothing proposition.

On the flip side, the owners may want to give a right to the deceased owner's spouse, children, or whomever else is a beneficiary to force a sale of their interest on the owners.

## Disability

Active owners need each other to run the business. If an owner becomes disabled with a chronic illness or injury, then the active owners have to shoulder the extra weight of the disabled owner. The active owners might not be able to support the disabled owner. The owners and company may want to give each other the option to purchase a disabled owner's interest to account for this change.

The owners will define disability, designate the party who declares a disability, and determine the length of the disability before the option is triggered. If the active owners or company exercise this right, they will be able to replace the disabled owner or continue the business without the disabled owner.

## Lost License

Some businesses such as professional firms require licensed owners. Some businesses depend on licensed owners even though a licensed owner is not required. If an owner loses his or her license, the other owners or company may want to have the right to buy the unlicensed owner's interest at a discounted price because it might affect the value of the company.

## Retirement

Some active owners may want to retire or quit working for the company. This might create tension between the retired owner and the active owners who are now carrying the weight of running the company. The owners may want to give each other and the company the right to purchase the interest of any owner who chooses to retire or quit.

## Divorces

The courts have a right to divide marital property. This includes an owner's interest in the company. This means you might end up with an ex-spouse as an owner in your company. The owners or the company may force an ex-spouse to sell his or her interest if the spouse signs the buy-sell agreement with this right. If you don't want to bother with getting the spouses of the owners to sign this agreement, you can always take your chance that an owner will not get divorced or that the judge will give the full interest to the owner and none to the ex-spouse.

## Bankruptcy

If an owner files for bankruptcy, the bankruptcy trustee can get the bankruptcy owner's interest in the company, then sell it to pay off creditors. In extreme cases the bankruptcy trustee can exercise the rights of the bankrupt owner and sell the company's assets or liquidate the company altogether to pay off creditors. The owners can agree that an owner who is about to file bankruptcy must provide notice to the other owners before filing for bankruptcy to give the other owners time to structure and force a sale of the bankrupt owner.

## Pledges

A pledge is an owner's use of his interest in the business as collateral on a loan. If he defaults on the loan, then the bank takes the interest. The owners may prohibit pledges, require consent for a pledge, or require the right to pay off the loan and take back the owner's pledged interest.

## Expulsion

Sometimes owners do bad things such as abuse drugs or alcohol, embezzle, or exhibit disturbing behavior. In these cases the other owners will want the option to expel the misbehaving owner and buy his interest at a discounted price.

# *Funding*

An event such as death, disability, expulsion, or decision to quit will either trigger an option to purchase, a right of first refusal, or the right to force a sale. The party with this right will then need to give notice of their decision to exercise that right. This means they're going to buy the other owner's interest. But where do these people or the company get the money to buy the interest?

Cash is one option. But that means that the company needs to keep cash on hand or that an owner needs to have enough cash to pay for the interest. Another option is a loan. But that assumes that the company or owner can get one. And who knows what interest rates will be like. The final option is owner financing. The owner buying the interest agrees to make a down payment (normally 20% to 30%) and then purchase the remaining amount in installments (normally three to five years).

There are other options for the events of death and disability. The company or each member may buy life insurance policies on each other to purchase the deceased member's interest. The company or its owners may also buy a disability insurance policy on its owners. You'll need to consider things such as the policy amount, the age of the owners, and various types of policies. You'll also need to consider the tax consequences of your decision. The same consideration applies to disability insurance which may cover the cost of a buyout when an owner is considered disabled.

# *Price*

How do you value a company when there's no public market to gauge price, especially for small businesses? It's not like you can input a bunch of numbers and variables and spit out a price. It's really worth what someone is willing to pay for it; which often means how much a buyer can afford, and what the return on their investment will be.

You can wait to set the price when an owner, ex-spouse, beneficiary, or a departing owner exercises a right to purchase. But this approach often ends with disputes and litigation. That's no way for a transaction to happen.

There's a number of other ways to set the price. Don't just pick one and stick with it throughout the life of the company. You'll want to adjust it as the company grows.

You could base the price on capital accounts, but they don't bear any relationship to the real worth of business.

You could base the price on a fixed price. That's seems easy enough. It's kind of like looking at the price tag on a product. This method might be a good candidate for a service business, a company in its first year, or a closely held business. But the value of a business fluctuates. Whatever price you choose will quickly be outdated. If you decide to go this route, then make sure to update the price every year or so. But most people forget to do this.

The other way to set the price is based on a formula. Here are a few to consider.

## Book Value

This sounds easy enough; just check the balance sheet and

you're good to go. But this formula doesn't account for intangible assets like reputation and goodwill. In some cases that's okay. It works well if you're just starting out or are marginally profitable in a highly competitive business. It doesn't work well for a profitable, mature company. If you go this route include a sample balance sheet to show how the book value is calculated.

## Multiple of Book Value

If you've built up some goodwill, have a positive reputation, or have a valuable asset such as a good lease, you can set the price at a multiple of book value. This might work for companies like a retail business and other companies not in the personalized service sector.

## Multiple of Earnings

This method takes the average of yearly earnings (three years is a good number) and chooses a multiplier. This method works well for businesses that have operated for a long time, have consistent profits, and have a good future. The multiplier depends on the industry, but normally is not higher than three. If you're one of those lucky businesses with great earnings, a niche, and a solid cash flow, you might be able to go as high as ten.

## Appraised Value

This method is simple. You hire a professional appraiser who decides the value. Or the buyer chooses an appraiser and the seller chooses an appraiser who each come up with a value on their own. If each of their appraisals are disparate, the two appraisers hire a third appraiser to provide the final value. This approach can be really expensive and take a lot of time. Since it's more art than science, it can also be subject to dispute. It's really only good for a company whose main asset is real property.

# *Ownership*

Let's take a look at the owners. If you're a majority owner, you may want your children to take over the business if you die or become disabled. You may also want to limit provisions that force you to sell your interest.

All owners need to keep an eye on changes in ownership percentage. Two minority interest owners may conspire to become majority owners and force another owner out.

An owner might not be active. If this is the case, then some provisions such as disability, divorce and others might not apply to them. Things change if you have silent owners.

Ownership is also affected by the party who purchases the interest. If the company purchases the interest with company funds, then the ownership adjusts accordingly and its funds are affected. If the company doesn't purchase the interest, then it's best to allow the owners to purchase the interest relative to their percentage ownership in the company.

# Buying and Selling Your Business

Money
Price
Entities or Assets
Due Diligence
People
Letter of Intent
Agreements
Closing

∾

If you're in the market to buy a business you can either buy a franchise or buy an existing business. Or you can just cut to the chase and start your own. If you're a business owner and want to sell, then you can place your business on the market and either sell your stock or membership in the company or you can sell its assets.

If you buy a franchise, you contact the franchisor, get a franchise disclosure document, and negotiate a franchise agreement. When the deal is done you'll have a license to use the franchisor's trademarks, operating manuals, advertising rights, exclusive geographic rights, and training benefits in exchange for a fee which is normally a percentage of the gross profits. Normally, a buyer sets up an LLC or corporation to run the franchise.

If you're a buyer and want to purchase an existing business, then you normally sign a confidentiality agreement, research the business, sometimes sign a letter of intent with the seller, negotiate a purchase and sale agreement, then close the deal.

# *Money*

If you're a buyer, it's a good idea to figure out the ballpark of how much you can afford. This will be a combination of how much you'll pay from your own savings, bank loans, and other financing methods along with how much cash the business can contribute to pay off the loan. There are a number of ways a buyer can pay for a business. The buyer can pay with cash, use savings, ask for help from family and friends, or get a bank loan.

Another option is owner financing where the buyer makes a down payment and signs a promissory note to pay the remaining amount. The seller secures the loan with cosigners on the note, a personal guarantee, first or second mortgages on the buyer's home or other real property, a security agreement on personal assets, the right to take back the lease, etc. What sort of security the seller asks for all depends on the buyer's financial strength. If the buyer defaults on the loan, the seller seizes and sells the secured assets to pay off the loan.

# *Price*

One of the first things a buyer and seller will need to do is arrive at a price. The buyer will want to kick the tires before the buyer offers or accepts a price. This means that the buyer will want to see the seller's tax returns, lease, title reports, environmental reports, contracts, account information, corporate or LLC records, licenses and permits, patents, copyrights, trademarks, financial statements, etc. The seller may provide these documents and information under the protection of a confidentiality agreement. This should protect the seller's interest and assuage concerns about releasing the documents and information.

The buyer will be ready to offer a price or consider the seller's price when the buyer has reviewed these documents and information. The price is an art. There's really no formula; well there *are* formulas, but formulas such as cap rate, book value, and multiples of book value only get you in the ballpark. The rest depends on the things such as the terms of the agreement, market demand, whether you're an investor, whether there is intellectual property, the value of goodwill, whether the business has valuable employees, whether the seller will remain as an employee, how much the buyer can afford, comparable business prices, etc. The buyer and seller can also agree to an earn-out agreement contingent on the success of the business after the sale.

Overall, price will be the biggest item in the negotiations. If the parties can't agree on price, then there will be no deal.

# *Entities or Assets*

You have two choices when you buy a business. You can either buy the assets (including trademarks, copyrights, liabilities, customer lists, etc.) or you can buy the stock if it's a corporation or the membership interest if it's an LLC. The buyer will more than likely want an asset sale. The advantages of buying the assets includes tax advantages with depreciation, the ability to exclude unattractive assets, removing the company's debts and liabilities from the deal, etc. The main disadvantages to an asset sale for a buyer is losing valuable assets such as a lease that can't be transferred to the new owner. If the buyer and seller agree to an asset sale, they will divide the assets and allocate a price to each one. The allocation affects depreciation and the cost basis of each asset.

But the seller will typically want to sell the entity to pay capital gains rates rather than income tax rates. If the seller is a corporation, the seller will want to avoid the huge hit that comes from double taxation.

Whatever the parties choose to do will affect the price. That's why this decision will need to be made early.

# *Due Diligence*

The buyer wants to make sure he or she knows what they're getting when they buy the business. No buyer wants surprises. The process of investigating the business is called due diligence. The documents and information the seller provides to the buyer under a confidentiality agreement is part of this process. But the buyer will want to look beyond these documents and information.

The buyer may search the recorder's offices to see if the assets are encumbered by any liens such as UCC finance statements, mechanic's liens, deeds of trust, etc. A title report will also show whether the property is owned free and clear or is subject to encumbrances. The buyer should search the court system records for any litigation and search other public records to make sure the company is in good standing. The buyer may get a Dun and Bradstreet report to find out the creditworthiness of the seller. Depending on the type of business, the buyer should search the records of other government agencies. The buyer will also want to ask for information on bank loans, money owed to suppliers, and potential claims. The buyer will ask the seller to represent the accuracy and completeness of these records along with other representations and warranties.

The seller will also want to check out the buyer, especially if the sale is owner financed. The seller can ask for financial statements, tax records, resumes, credit reports, references, court records, and some of the same records the buyer will review. The seller will also want representations and warranties from the buyer. If you're the seller and are financing the transaction, then you want to make sure that you're first in line as a creditor or if you're second in line, that there will be enough left over for you.

The seller and buyer will need to respond to the results of the due diligence. This may mean adjusting the price, carving out liabilities, including indemnification language, etc. Whatever is done, the agreement is only as good as the financial soundness of the seller or buyer.

# *People*

The people in the business are just as important as the assets, stock, or membership interest. Sometime the buyer will want to keep an owner as a consultant, a part-time or full-time employee, or an advisor. The buyer might want to consider a transition period for an owner. This requirement can either be included in the business sale agreement or negotiated separately. If an ex-owner becomes an employee, then treat him or her as you would any other employee by providing an employment contract or an at-will offer. Make sure to specify their duties. If the ex-owner is a consultant, then make sure to negotiate an independent contractor agreement.

Sometimes the business will have key employees that the buyer wants to keep. If the key employee has a contract, the buyer might just take over their contract. If it's an entity sale, the contract will automatically be part of the deal. If it's an asset sale, then the parties need to get proper consent to assign the contract to the buyer.

Sometime the seller's owners will have no part in the business once it transfers to the buyer. If this is the case, the buyer should consider a non-compete agreement to protect itself from future competition. The seller might start a competing business or work for a competitor. The non-compete normally covers a geographic area (these days that might include the internet), the type of activities, and the duration of the non-compete. The non-compete can be part of the business sale agreement or a separate document.

# *Letters of Intent*

The buyer and seller may consider entering into a letter of intent some time after they sign a confidentiality agreement but before they sign a business purchase agreement. When the parties reach this point they can go ahead and sign a letter of intent or they can immediately start negotiating the business sale agreement.

Typically the parties will choose to sign a non-binding letter of intent if: they don't want to take their chances that one of the parties will change the basic terms; they want to exclusively negotiate a deal; or they want to create a moral obligation to negotiate a deal in good faith. The letter of intent should be non-binding. Otherwise it makes sense to just negotiate the final business sale agreement.

Be careful in how you word the letter. Otherwise you might end up with a binding agreement when you didn't intend to have one. The letter can include things such as price, a list of assets to be purchased, how to handle liabilities, whether the parties will exclusively negotiate with each other, negotiation schedules, further investigations, and whatever else the parties want to include so long as you don't include too many details to make it a binding agreement.

# *Agreements*

The business sale agreement is the last step before closing the deal. It's the document that puts your agreement in writing. An asset agreement and a stock or membership interest purchase agreement are essentially the same, except for a few key differences. The business sale agreement includes many extra terms including the parties, sales price, assets or business purchase identification, payment terms, liabilities, representations, closing terms, dispute resolution procedures and many more provisions.

If the sale is owner financed, the parties will also need a promissory note, security agreement, UCC financing statements, deed of trust, etc. If the owner provides services to the buyer, the owner will need an employment agreement, consulting agreement, or offer letter depending on what the owner will do. If the owner does not provide services, the parties will need to consider a non-compete agreement.

If the sale is an asset sale, then the parties will need a bill of sale to transfer the assets from the seller to the buyer. They will also need to assign leases, other contracts, and the rights to intellectual property such as copyrights, trademarks, and patents.

The buyer and seller should not rely on each other's oral promises. Everything should be in writing.

# *Closing*

The closing is when all the parties who have the authority to sign the documents meet and finalize the transaction. This can take place at the business, an attorney's office, or somewhere where it's easy to make copies and last minute changes. When all the documents are signed, the buyer walks away with a business and the seller walks away with cash or rights to receive cash.

# Author: Andrew C. Mitton

Andrew C. Mitton is Alaska's small business attorney. He's worked in law firms and large Alaska Native corporations for more than 12 years. Throw in another year on top of that working for a judge.

During that time he negotiated and drafted hundreds of contracts, managed many business acquisitions, managed the corporate records for more than 60 companies, designed and developed a compliance and ethics program covering more than 1,500 employees, argued a matter in front of the Alaska Supreme Court, and taught himself web design.

Mr. Mitton founded Vellum LLC in 2011 to design online legal systems and provide legal services to the small business owner.

# *Attorneys*

The person writing this book is an attorney, which means I'm biased. So when it comes to the question of whether you need an attorney, I'll just give you your options and let you choose.

## Option 1
No attorney. Figure things out on your own. There are lots of self-help books that will save you money.

## Option 2
Online services/no attorney. You can go online and find plenty of companies who will give you the forms you need. They're all over the place. Some might even have an attorney on call to answer your questions.

## Option 3
A local attorney. You can look through you phone book or ask around and find an attorney.

## Option 4
Vellum LLC. Vellum's Inside-out Legal Services™ are unlike any other law firm or attorney that I'm aware of.

My opinion: Many people are very capable of teaching themselves, but I've seen too many instances when someone tried to do things on their own and their lack of experience cost them dearly in the long run. It's not good to be penny-wise and pound foolish. The other problem is that there is a lot to learn. To learn everything you need to know about LLCs, trademarks, employment law, and selling a business, takes a long time. The biggest cost is your time. But some people have done it on their own just fine.

The online systems do a fine job for some people. But they're mostly national companies who don't have experience with Alaska and its laws. They mostly provide a one-size-fits all approach. It's like walking into JC Penny to buy a suit and finding out that they only have one size. The suit will fit a small part of the population, but the rest get a suit that's either too big or too small.

Local attorneys are familiar with Alaska, but they are expensive. Most attorneys cut and paste old documents and take a long time to do it, so you're paying for their inefficiency. There are a couple of attorneys who have tried to automate things, but their efforts involve a paralegal whose salary is worked into the price you pay. I've yet to meet an attorney or law firm who has created any sort of full-fledged automated system.

That's where Vellum LLC and Inside-out Legal Services™ comes into play. Vellum's system allows you to do most of the work on your own, but with attorney oversight. And Vellum passes the cost savings to you.

You get the peace and comfort of knowing that an attorney reviewed your work, caught any errors, and has optimized things for your situation. And it all comes from a local attorney that you can meet with personally. It's like having your very own legal department without the cost.

www.ingramcontent.com/pod-product-compliance
Lightning Source LLC
Chambersburg PA
CBHW060542100426
42742CB00013B/2416